THE PRACTICAL ART OF

Baby Massage

PERSEUS PUBLISHING

CAMBRIDGE, MASSACHUSETTS

For Harley and Sauri

Created and produced by
CARROLL & BROWN LIMITED
20 Lonsdale Road
Queen's Park
London NW6 6RD

EDITOR Dawn Henderson
DESIGNER Evie Loizides
ART EDITOR Tracy Timson
PHOTOGRAPHY Jules Selmes

Printed and bound by Bookprint, S.L., Barcelona

ISBN 1-55561-341-1

Perseus Publishing is a member of the Perseus Books Group

Find us on the World Wide Web at http://www.perseuspublishing.com

Perseus Publishing books are available at special discounts
for bulk purchases in the U.S. by corporations, institutions,
and other organizations. For more information, please
contact the Special Markets Department at the Perseus
Books Group, 11 Cambridge Center, Cambridge, MA
02142, or call (617) 252-5298.

Foreword

The most powerful massage that your baby will ever receive during his lifetime is birth itself. At this time, the prolonged contractions of the uterus push the baby out through the birth canal, stimulating his peripheral nervous system and major organs in preparation for life outside the womb. By continuing this physical stimulation as your baby develops, you are following nature's way of boosting your baby's resilience.

The techniques in this book are specifically devised to give you and your baby all the benefits of orthodox massage, while helping your baby to fulfill his physical potential at each phase of development—from birth through to walking. Acting on both the muscles and the joints, these techniques convey all the benefits of a loving touch and also ensure that your baby achieves full flexibility as he prepares for mobility. Practiced consistently, these massage techniques also give you the opportunity to check that there are no areas of hidden tension or stiffness in your baby's muscles and joints so that you can secure the full structural health and fitness of your baby. And they ensure a level of relaxation that means that—both physically and emotionally— your baby is "trauma free," maintains good posture, and enjoys the self-confidence that accompanies a wide range of physical movement.

Massage is medicine and it is one of the most useful skills that a parent can acquire. It is immediate, convenient, and both preventative and curative. It can be used to alleviate minor ailments and bring an element of relief and comfort to children with special needs.

Massage will add a whole new dimension to your relationship with your child.

Contents

Contents

Introduction

Baby Massage begins by introducing you to massage—telling you all you need to know about why and how to massage your baby. You can see the many benefits of massaging your child and learn the foundation of good massage practice.

Chapter one shows you how to get in touch with your baby from birth and use massage to develop a close relationship with your child from the very early stages. It gives advice on how to enhance your relationship in your baby's early weeks and help her to thrive.

Chapter two introduces an effective massage routine which, when practiced regularly, will promote emotional security alongside all the prime physical attributes that constitute good posture, health, and fitness. These unique combinations of massage will enable you to promote and maintain your baby's strength and suppleness. The techniques can also bring to light and help to alleviate any hidden areas of muscular tension and joint inflexibility.

Taking massage through to early childhood, chapter three explores the role of massage in helping your baby to secure and maintain a healthy and comfortable sitting posture.

As your baby becomes more mobile she will not wish to remain still for long periods and, therefore, massage can become increasingly difficult. This is the time to engage your baby in movement. Chapter four provides soft gymnastic games designed to maintain existing

suppleness and promote strength, balance, as well as good posture—both sitting and standing.

In chapter five, *Baby Massage* covers some of the most common complaints and shows how massage and movement can be used to prevent and alleviate some of these disorders. Special needs are also discussed, with advice on how massage can complement existing forms of treatment and therapy.

Lastly, at the back of the book you can discover how, after a period without massage, you can reintroduce techniques to your child when the time is right.

Throughout the book, babies are described as either "he" or "she" depending on the sex of the baby featured in the routine.

HOW TO USE THE BOOK

- The left page of each exercise explains the purpose and the benefits of the massage, and the right page shows you how to do it, step by step.
- Boxed text highlights any important issues or contraindications to bear in mind while you massage your baby.

When to massage

Until your baby is used to being massaged, choosing the right time to massage him can make all the difference as to whether or not he will enjoy it. There are several factors to take into consideration when you are planning your baby's massage sessions.

• It is always best to massage your baby between feeds. If he is too full, the process can be uncomfortable, especially when you are massaging his belly, or laying him on his front to massage his back. Also, if your baby is hungry he is unlikely to tolerate being massaged for any length of time.

• A good time to massage is last thing at night, after your baby has had a bath, or any time during the day when he is at his most relaxed and responsive.

• Make sure that your home is quiet, so that you can focus on the massage completely.

• Try to be consistent with the timing of your massage, so that your baby will learn to anticipate and look forward to the sessions.

WHEN NOT TO MASSAGE

• With the exception of the massages specifically designed to alleviate the symptoms of illness, do not massage your baby if he is unwell. In most cases, babies who are feeling ill just want to sleep and be held.

• You should never massage your baby against his will and it is always best not to wake him for a massage.

• Do not massage your baby with oil if he has a skin condition, as the oil may exacerbate it. Consult your pediatrician for advice and a suitable alternative.

• If your baby has been immunized, wait for 48 hours to find out how he has been affected. Avoid the site of the injection, but if it leaves a hard lump, you can gently knead it away between your thumb and forefinger once it is no longer sensitive.

• Avoid any areas of your baby's body that are bruised, swollen, at all inflamed, or acutely sensitive. Instead consult your physician.

The benefits of touch

Touch is the newborn's first language—it is her prime means of communication and plays an essential role in the forming of early parent–child relationships. Massaging your baby allows you to express emotional affection and to fulfill your baby's need for physical contact. The benefits of massage are both emotional and physical, so your baby will achieve all-around wellbeing.

EMOTIONAL

With every emotional change there is a muscular reaction. By easing muscular tension, baby massage calms the emotions and helps to relieve some of the trauma and anxiety associated with birth, a new environment, and weaning. There is also a variety of other emotional benefits:

- Massaging your baby introduces a unique level of confidence and trust to your relationship.
- As fathers generally need experience in handling their babies, massaging will bring them more in touch. Massage provides fathers with the opportunity to strengthen their relationship and learn how to handle their babies with confidence.
- Regular massage reduces the circulation of cortisol in the bloodstream, a stress hormone—this reduction is constant and maintained between massage sessions.
- Massage stimulates the release of the body's natural opiates—endorphins—which subdue pain. Together with the reductions of cortisol, this induces general feelings of wellbeing throughout your baby's body.
- As you massage your baby, you also maintain eye-contact, kissing, stroking, and vocalizing, which encourage closeness in a relationship. Massaging your baby promotes attachment.

To touch is also to be touched—when you touch your baby you cannot fail to be touched by your baby in return.

Baby massage encourages muscular coordination and can help your baby to open and straighten her arms and legs and let go of her tendency to return to the fetal posture during the early months.

PHYSICAL

The skin provides the central nervous system with a continual stream of information about the body's immediate environment. As you touch your baby's skin, the sensation is relayed to her central nervous system, which initiates physical, physiological and emotional responses. Other physical benefits of massage include:

• Every bit as important as vitamins, minerals, and proteins, touch is essential to the healthy growth and development of your baby—babies who are deprived of human touch do not thrive.
• A regular massage encourages the increase of growth hormones from the pituitary gland.
• As muscles relax, they absorb blood and when they contract, they help to pump blood back to the heart and aid the venous return. The periphery of your baby's body—the top of her head, her hands, and her feet—is often cold as her circulatory system is not fully developed. Baby massage aids circulation—your baby's hands and feet become warm as you massage.
• As muscles relax, they allow the free movement of the body's joints. Baby massage encourages muscular

relaxation and joint flexibility at the stage when your baby is stretching to establish a wide range of physical movement and mobility.
• Regular massage cleanses your baby's skin and helps to remove dead cells. It opens the pores and encourages the elimination of toxins and the secretion of sebum—the natural oil that aids the skin's elasticity and resilience and resistance to infections.
• Massage stimulates the vagus nerve, one branch of which leads to the gastro-intestinal tract, where it facilitates the release of food absorption hormones such as insulin and glucose.
• Massage and movement both promote the flow of waste-removing lymphatic fluid and improve the body's resistance to infection.
• A loving touch makes us feel better. The Hippocratic—or ancient Greek first medical—definition of good health is "a good bodily feeling."

What you will need

Treat your massage sessions as special times for you and your baby and create a pleasant environment for the massage. Set out the things you will need:

- If your room is not carpeted, use a blanket and a cushion to sit on and lay a soft towel over a sheepskin or a folded blanket for your baby. She will not feel comfortable on a hard surface, particularly if she lacks head control— she could bump her head. If your room is carpeted, use a large folded towel for your baby.
- Use a bowl for your oil, even if it is in a container, as it can be easily spilled. Make sure that the bowl is within reaching distance, so that you can replenish your oil during the massage.
- You may find that some soft music sets a relaxing mood.
- Keep a diaper and a fresh towel handy in case there are any little accidents during the massage.

Always "skin test" the oil you intend to use. Rub a little into a small area of skin on your baby's calf or the top of her arm, and wait for 30 minutes to see if there is any allergic reaction. This usually takes the form of red blotches, which will disappear after an hour or two. Should this happen, try another oil or ask your pediatrician for an alternative.

- Finally, your baby may well wish to feed after her massage, so if you are bottle-feeding, have a bottle prepared and close at hand.

OILS

Your baby's skin is fine and sensitive, with far more nerve endings than that of any adult. The constant regeneration of healthy cells keeps the baby's skin smooth and moist and a regular massage with an appropriate oil will also cleanse the skin's pores of its dead cells and give it a healthy glow. The oil that you use should allow your hands to glide easily and enable you to give a little depth to your massage without discomfort. It should not feel too sticky or greasy, it should be pure in its content and whenever possible, organic.

Here are the best base massage oils— all are inexpensive and widely available:

- Grapeseed Known for its purity and easy absorption.
- Sweet Almond Light but also slightly more dense.
- Olive oil Rich and good for dry skin.
- Sunflower oil (organic only) Fine and recommended for use when massaging premature babies.

Natural fruit or vegetable oils are readily absorbed through the surface of the skin, so keep replenishing as you massage. Never pour any oil back into the bottle, as it may cause contamination.

*Essential oils are for external use only.
They should not be used as a substitute for a professional
diagnosis and treatment. Always consult your doctor if you think
your baby is ill.*

AROMATHERAPY OILS

Also known as essential oils, these are highly refined oils that possess the scent and the healing properties of the plant, flower, or herb from which they were extracted. They can be used to enhance mood—to relax or invigorate—or to treat specific ailments. The oils are highly potent, however, and are not recommended for use with very young babies. After the age of about two months, they can be effective, but they should only be used if they are well diluted in a good base massage oil (see above)—3 drops of essential oil to 2 tablespoons of base massage oil. Your baby is very sensitive to smell, so check that he has a positive emotional reaction to the blend.

You may want to put two or three drops of essential oil into your baby's bath. Dilute the oil in a tablespoonful of milk first, so that it dissolves more easily.

You could also use an essential oil burner, which will diffuse the oil's effects into the atmosphere.

Not all essential oils are suitable for babies but some of the most useful and effective are:

TEA TREE Recommended for skin infections, this is non-toxic and antiseptic.

CAMOMILE ROMAN Calming and soothing, this oil aids digestion and soothes irritability (see page 80).

LAVENDER This antiseptic oil is good for soothing and healing minor burns and bites. It can also be used as a chest or nasal decongestant (page 74).

EUCALYPTUS A powerful decongestant that can be used for a chest and back massage (see page 74) to relieve coughs, colds, and congestion. Don't use this oil, however, if your baby is having homeopathic treatment.

FRANKINCENSE Deeply relaxing with a very pleasant aroma, it can also be used for a chest massage (page 36) to deepen the breathing rhythm and soothe discomfort.

ROSE OTTO This is recommended for use with dry skin. It has a beautiful aroma, but is also expensive.

Do not use essential oils if your child suffers from any major disease or disorder. Consult your doctor first.

Good massage techniques

When you massage your baby, you need to keep your hands open and relaxed and make contact with your baby's skin with your fingers and your palms. If your hands are at all stiff or your touch is hesitant, you may transfer tension to your baby, so try to remain relaxed and confident throughout.

As your baby develops and enjoys a more formal massage routine, you can increase the pressure slightly to give a little more depth to your touch. This gives your baby an important message—he is resilient. The more confident your touch, the more confidence you instill in your baby. And as your baby develops, you may need to increase the speed of your strokes to hold his attention and keep him engaged.

Punctuate your massage with lots of hugs and kisses, talk and sing to your baby and enjoy it. Babies love to play—this is how they learn best. As soon as you start to get too serious, your baby will lose interest in the massage and disengage.

Keep your hands on your baby's skin as much as you can and if you stop to turn a page in this book, or to replenish your oil, keep one hand resting upon your baby's body.

The way in which you use your hands is very important and will make all the difference to the effectiveness of your baby's massage.

The strokes themselves are not difficult to learn and you will soon be doing them intuitively. Rub your hands together and give them a shake to warm them and loosen them up before you start. Keep your hands relaxed from your wrists. The main terms to look out for are as follows:

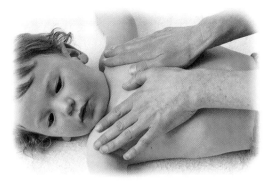

Rubbing

Pressing gently and moving the relaxed weight of your hand or hands backward and forward over your baby's body or limb.

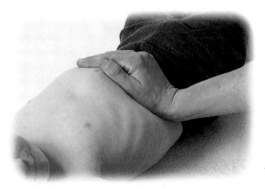

Kneading

Squeezing and releasing the soft parts of your baby's body gently with your whole hand.

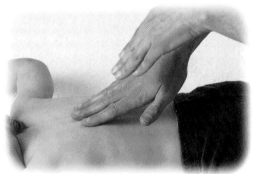

Stroking

Moving the relaxed weight of your whole hand across the surface of your baby's body.

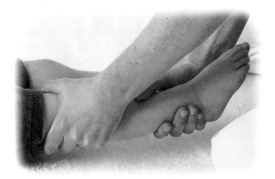

Hand-over-hand

Beginning a movement with one hand as you cease the same movement with the other hand.

Percussion

Using the relaxed weight of your cupped hands to tap rhythmically the front or back of the body.

Before you begin

When you are preparing to massage, make sure that you are calm and focused—if you are distracted or hurried, your baby will not feel relaxed. If your baby does not immediately seem to respond well, persevere—three or four sessions is usually all it takes for babies to begin enjoying massage. Remember, you do not need to practice the whole of a sequence straight away. Stop when your baby wants to and build on your routine little by little every time you do it.

• Use a warm, draft-free room in which you can remain uninterrupted for about an hour.
• Wear comfortable, loose-fitting clothes.
• Wash your hands, make sure that they are not cold and that you have on no jewelry that could scratch your baby's skin.
• Lay your baby on a soft, warm surface, such as a thick warm cotton towel— avoid wool, which can irritate oily skin.
• Keep your bowl of massage oil within easy reach.

When you start, the most important thing to do is to relax and have fun. Massage is meant to be extremely pleasurable for you both. If your baby does not respond well, stop, give her a feed or a cuddle and then try again. Those babies that resist massage are often the ones that actually need it the most and end up enjoying it the most.

While you massage your baby:

• Keep your touch rhythmic and put your mind in your hands. Put aside worries and focus on what you are doing as you do it.

If you find sitting on the floor uncomfortable, you could massage your baby on a bed.

Sit on the edge of a cushion with your legs and feet open in front of you.

- Talk and sing to your baby and try to maintain eye-contact.
- Always stop if your baby cries. This is something that you do with your baby, not to your baby.
- If your baby does not respond well, you could try massaging her clothed at first.

It is important that you remain relaxed and that your position is comfortable while you are massaging your baby. The following positions can be fairly easily maintained, but however you sit, make sure that you can lean forward without straining your back. If you do find that you become uncomfortable at any point during a massage, pause and change your position.

Kneel down and sit comfortably on your feet on a cushion with your knees open. Relax your arms and shoulders.

15

Introducing your baby to massage

Key benefits

- Closeness and contentment between mother and baby.
- Learning how and where your baby likes to be stroked.
- Making your baby feel protected and loved. Strengthening the physical and emotional bond between father and baby.
- Skin-to-skin physical contact between parent and baby.
- Nurturing your baby's feelings of security.
- Aiding digestion.
- Strengthening your baby's immune system.

All mothers want to hold their babies before they are weighed, measured, bathed, or dressed and establish skin-to-skin contact. Touch is the primal language of the newborn and it is through holding and caressing that a baby is made to feel welcomed and loved. This maternally sensitive period—both physically and emotionally—immediately following the baby's birth is one to welcome the new baby quite literally into the bosom of the family. For those mothers and babies who miss this period, however, this can also be created at a later time.

Although the need to be held, stroked, and touched continues throughout our lives, it is at its most intense in infancy during the pre-verbal period. In many other cultures and other countries—such as India, Africa, and South East Asia—babies are massaged daily from the time of their birth and although this is sometimes the role of the midwife, it can be done more easily and with even more benefits, by the baby's own mother.

Most very young babies feel uncomfortable and over-exposed when they are naked, so now is the time for gentle, non-intrusive caresses, rather than a more structured massage. In these early days of your baby's life, be guided by intuition, first holding and rocking and then stroking and getting the feel of your young baby. Your baby will soon "grow into" his massage routines, so at this stage, use touch to instill confidence, trust, and affection.

Sleeping and waking

Newborn babies usually spend most of their time sleeping—maybe as many as 18 hours a day! There are five different states of sleep and wakefulness which tend to occur in cycles of about two hours—newborn babies have no sense of day and night. The cycle goes from deep sleep to light sleep to fussing, feeding, and then to light wakefulness, after which the baby becomes drowsy again and drops back into deep sleep.

From about six to eight weeks your baby will still sleep for something like 15 hours a day and more of these hours may be concentrated around night-time. It may be some time, however, before your baby will "sleep through" the night—this usually starts to happen after about 12 months.

When your baby has woken, having fed, and settled into a quiet state of wakefulness, you can start to introduce massage, first by developing your sense of touch. These are the times when you should be guided by your

intuition and your baby's responses—remember, he is still getting used to his new world. Trying to massage your baby when he does not respond well will be of no benefit to either of you.

As time goes on, your baby's periods of wakefulness will become longer and so your opportunities for massage will be greater. But getting your baby used to being touched and stroked at this stage will help to make a more formal massage routine far easier to introduce. Use the strokes described below to develop feelings of closeness and contentment with your baby.

Look into your baby's eyes as you caress him and keep your movements slow and relaxed.

1

Lay down on your left side, with your baby facing you, lying on his right side. Stroke your baby with the whole of your right hand, from the back of his neck to the base of his spine—in the same way as you would stroke a kitten or a puppy.

• *Continue for about a minute.*

2

Use a circular movement to gently massage around your baby's upper back and then right down the length of his back to the base of his spine.

• *Continue for about a minute.*

3

Next, slowly take the movement to his arm. Keep your touch gentle and relaxed as you take the stroke from his shoulder to his hand.

• *Continue for about a minute. Repeat with his right arm.*

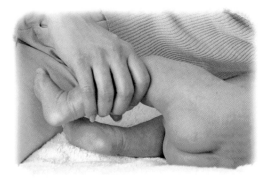

4

Move your hand to the top of your baby's leg and stroke down from his hip to his foot with your palm. You can give his leg a little gentle shake to loosen it up and help him to relax.

• *Continue for about a minute. Repeat with his right leg.*

Crying

All babies cry—it is their method of communicating with their parents and letting them know how they feel. During the first six weeks of your baby's life, the amount of time she spends crying may increase as her desire to communicate with you grows. You will learn to interpret her cries and identify when she is hungry, when she is uncomfortable, and when she is lonely.

At times, your baby may seem to cry for no reason—she has been fed, changed, and cuddled but continues to be upset. These seemingly inexplicable episodes of crying are usually because your baby needs close physical contact and wants to be held. Here, the power of touch can be very effective. Learning how your baby likes to be stroked and where she enjoys it the most can make soothing easier.

This sort of comfort begins by building up a series of caresses that make your baby feel protected and loved. Be calm in your movements and light in your touch—and if your baby does not respond well, refer to the Tiger in the tree massage on page 84.

A cry for food usually begins with whimpering, then becomes rhythmic; an angry cry is loud and intense; and a cry of pain is sudden. You will soon learn to interpret your own baby's cries.

Once you have established that your baby's tears are not the result of hunger, discomfort, or illness, sit comfortably with your baby and try laying her on her belly over your knees. Stroke down her back and legs slowly and gently to soothe her.

Feeding

Given the normal two-hour cycle of your new baby's day, she may eat as many as ten times a day. As a rule, it is best to massage your baby between feeds, when she is neither full nor hungry. You can, however, guide your baby to feed and encourage her to "latch on"—whether you are breast-feeding or bottle-feeding. It is best not to distract your baby while she is nursing, although some mothers intuitively stroke their babies' heads and backs. Parent and baby eye-contact can be at its most rewarding as you satisfy your baby's hunger. It is no coincidence that a new baby's focused vision is restricted to 14 inches—the distance between a mother's breast and face. And this intimacy can be shared as you bottle-feed your baby in the crook of your arm at breast level.

Regular massage stimulates appetite and aids digestion. Babies massaged regularly can gain weight faster than those who are not.

Guidance

If you are breast-feeding, you could try stroking your baby's cheek with your nipple and when her mouth is open wide, bring her to your breast.

If your baby is having problems feeding, try altering her position when she feeds—she may need to be more upright, sitting chest-to-chest with her chin to your breast.

If you are worried about your baby's weight or have any problems with feeding, always seek professional advice. Feeding should be comfortable and enjoyable for both of you.

Father and baby

Supporting your baby at the base of the spine and the back of the head is a secure and comfortable position in which to establish eye-contact.

Fathers don't experience the nine months of physical closeness that a mother shares with her baby during that first period of growth and development inside her body. Some mothers say that they "know" the very moment they conceive; others, that they feel the baby "fluttering" during the early weeks. Later, of course, movements are felt more and more intensely as the baby turns and presses against the walls of the uterus.

The first time a father comes into direct physical contact with his baby is usually at the birth, when the newborn child is handed to him. Touching and holding such a tiny person can be a daunting experience, and it is important for both father and baby to be given plenty of opportunity to "get in touch" with each other.

Fathers benefit from time spent with their babies, and massage can help to develop their touch and handling skills. This massage routine fosters trust between father and child and increases a father's confidence in his ability to change and bathe the baby and to help more with the daily responsibilities of childcare. Massage will also help to strengthen the physical and emotional relationship between a father and his baby. By learning how to handle his child better, a father is more able to soothe and comfort his baby at times when the baby's mother needs to take a break.

You can adapt the movements for any occasion when you are just sitting with your baby. Stroke her back and around her neck and shoulders as she sits on your lap.

*Make sure that you are
laying comfortably and that
your shoulders are relaxed
throughout the massage.*

1

Lay down on your side with
your baby facing you, laying on
her side. Using the relaxed
weight of your whole right hand,
start stroking your baby's upper
back in a circular motion.

2

Then, take this
movement down the
length of your baby's
spine smoothly, to
include your baby's
lower back.

3

Using the palm of your
hand, gently stroke all
around the crown of your
baby's head in a slow,
circular motion.

• *Repeat for as long as
your baby is relaxed and
comfortable.*

Belly time

For your young baby, regular waking time spent laying belly-down ensures the structural health and fitness of his body in a way no other natural position can achieve. When your baby lies on his belly, he lifts his head to look around him—strengthening the supporting muscles in his neck. Once he has comfortably reached this stage, he will then lift his head and shoulders, developing strength in his arms and shoulders and flexibility in his spine.

Allowing your baby to spend more waking time on his belly will also make it easier for him to crawl. Babies who do not lay on their bellies usually develop later than those who do.

Having achieved this, he will then raise his head and shoulders even further. This stretches open your baby's chest—so that he achieves a deeper breathing rhythm and maximizes his lung capacity.

A deeper breathing rhythm is of great benefit to the heart and lungs. The increase of oxygen will also boost all the other major organs and your baby's immune system. And as his chest stretches open, so, too, does his abdominal cavity—aiding digestion.

To complete this gradual phase of development, your baby will lift his head, chest, arms and shoulders and, ultimately, his legs and feet in a unique display of strength and flexibility. It is important to encourage your baby to spend some waking time lying on his belly, so if your baby initially finds it uncomfortable, use the following technique.

Advice given to parents to counteract the incidence of cot death includes avoiding laying your baby on his belly to sleep. Regular periods of waking time spent laying on his belly, however, are of great importance to the development of your child.

Belly time

1

Sit comfortably against a wall with your knees bent. Lay your baby belly-forward on your thighs, with his knees open and his feet together. Your baby's feet should be pressed together, so that he cannot push against you and propel himself over your knees.

2

Stroke your baby's back, hand-over-hand, and make him feel comfortable in this position, then very gradually lower your knees.

3

Keep bringing your knees down very slowly until your baby is eventually laying flat on your thighs.

4

When your baby is comfortable with this, you can lay him on the floor on his belly, with his chest and shoulders supported on a cushion. Soon you will be able to remove the cushion, giving your baby the full benefits of time on his belly.

Full massage routine

Key benefits

- Maintaining balance and posture.
- Muscular coordination and suppleness.
- Joint flexibility.
- Releasing any hidden areas of tension in muscles and joints.
- Strengthening the back.
- Digestion—encouraging the belly to relax.
- Enhancing wellbeing by maximizing breathing potential.
- Will help your baby to thrive.
- Physical alignment and internal energy flow.
- Exposing skin to light and oxygen.

From about two months of age, your baby should be feeling a little less vulnerable. It is likely that she will feel happy to remain naked and has lost some of the physiological flexion that kept her arms and legs tucked into her body in a semi-fetal posture as a newborn. When she has reached this stage, you can start to introduce the following "toe-to-top" massage routine, which will help her to achieve her maximum potential at each phase of development during the following months.

Most babies prefer massage to begin with their feet and legs and continue up the body, as this is a non-invasive and gradual approach, which allows your baby to get used to the routine. Starting at her feet and continuing fluidly up her body, this comprehensive sequence of massage techniques can secure your baby's full structural health and fitness. It encourages the flexibility of all of her major joints, relaxes her muscles, and will provide her with a solid foundation for good posture and later mobility.

The routine should be practiced regularly—every day if possible—giving you and your baby a regular period of special time and closeness. Choose the time of day when your baby is at her best—not too full, too hungry, or too tired. Above all else, this is something you do with your baby, not to your baby, so take your cues from her and punctuate your massage with lots of hugs and kisses.

You do not have to perform the sequence all in one go—introduce a little at a time—but aim to graduate to a full session. The separate massage techniques are designed to interlink, so that every part of your baby's body is addressed.

Feet...

Foot massage is one of the oldest forms of massage and can be extremely relaxing for the whole body. Your baby will find it pleasurable and it will also help with her balance and posture as she spreads her toes, extends her heels, and opens her feet.

The soles of your baby's feet are very sensitive and stroking them will provoke a reflex—she will curl her toes. As a result, you should concentrate on the less ticklish tops and sides of the feet. Stroking the top of her toes and the outer side of her ankles will encourage your baby to extend her toes, so focus on these areas for the best effect.

When your baby gets a little older and starts walking, you should allow her to enjoy the freedom of being barefooted for the first six weeks before putting her in shoes, so that her feet can develop, spread, and assume their natural shape. To stand with confidence and security, your baby's heels must be well-grounded. This is why it is best not to encourage your baby to stand on tiptoes—the more she stands on her toes, the more insecure she will feel and the more difficult she will find it to balance. The following technique will help your baby to open her feet and bring down her heels in preparation for standing—this is particularly important if her feet tend to turn inward.

As it is relatively unobtrusive, you can massage your baby's feet anywhere you happen to be sitting together—even when she is wearing socks. Rubbing your baby's feet can also be soothing when she is unwell.

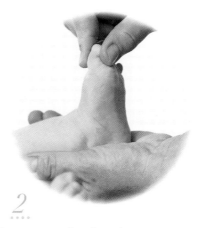

1

Make sure that your hands are well-oiled. Begin to knead and rub the top of your baby's foot with your hands.

• *Continue for 2–3 minutes.*

2

Then, start to roll each toe between your forefinger and thumb and gently separate the toes so that they fan out slightly.

• *Continue for about 20 seconds.*

3

Now pull the whole foot smoothly, hand-over-hand, through your palms. You will probably need to replenish your oil at this stage of the massage.

• *Continue for about 20 seconds.*

4

Flex your baby's ankle and extend the heel of her foot by turning her foot outward with one hand while you rub her calf with the other.

• *Continue for about 20 seconds. Repeat with the other foot.*

Full massage routine

...to legs...

From about two months, your baby will begin to exercise his legs vigorously, kicking and stretching them daily for hours on end in a wonderful display of aerobics. This develops the strength and coordination of his postural muscles—the calves, thighs, and buttocks—and secures and maintains the flexibility of his hips and knees. The strength and coordination of these muscles and the flexibility of these joints will provide your baby with a strong foundation for upright postures and a wide variety of movement.

Both sitting and standing involve balance and this is made far easier when flexible joints provide your baby with a broad base. Your

baby will develop the self-confidence to stand tall with the inner feeling that the foundations of his body—his legs—are both strong and flexible.

Massaging your baby's legs will help to promote the development of coordination, strengthen his lower back, and maintain the flexibility of his knees and ankles. It will also ensure that there are no areas of hidden tension or stiffness in any of his muscles and joints.

These massage techniques will leave your baby's legs completely relaxed and supple.

30

1

Hold both of your baby's legs by the ankles and loosen them up a little by gently "bicycling" them, bending and straightening them alternately.

• *Continue for about 20 seconds.*

2

Then put your left hand at the top of your baby's right leg and pull through your well-oiled palms from his thigh downward in a hand-over-hand movement, right down to his foot.

• *Repeat 4–5 times.*

3

Hold your baby's right ankle in your right hand and massage his thigh with your left hand. Massage up the front, then down the back of his thigh.

• *Repeat 4–5 times.*

4

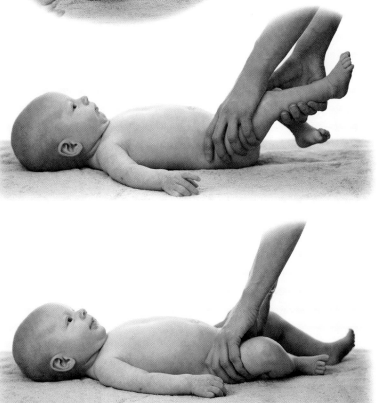

Now, pull the whole leg again from the thigh to the foot hand-over-hand.

• *Repeat the sequence with your baby's left leg.*

5

Shake your baby's legs and rest your hands on his inner thighs. Turn your hands outward and pull down the back of his knees and calves—he will straighten his legs. Keep gliding your hands up the front and down the back of his legs.

• *Repeat 4–5 times.*

...to hips...

The flexibility of your baby's hips is crucial for good posture, because these are the joints that support her spine and pelvis. Hip mobility is also very important for all-around lower-body suppleness.

Babies enjoy an incredible range of hip movements—they can put their toes in their mouths quite effortlessly. As time goes on, however, most lose this wonderful flexibility. Massaging your baby's hips will help her to maintain the flexibility of these joints as she grows and strengthens. Consistent practice will ensure that your baby can continue to enjoy a wide variety of movements as she strengthens and maintain good posture, both sitting and standing.

Although your baby's hips will have been examined at birth, you can make sure that they are developing healthily by checking that they do not "clunk" when she moves, that she can freely open her knees sideways, that both knees look the same when held together and bent, and that the two little creases at the bottom of her spine are uniform when she lays down on her belly.

Be sure to perform the steps in the order they are given. Never force any of the movements and if your baby finds any of the positions uncomfortable, consult your pediatrician.

Babies who practice standing before they are sitting properly are more prone to hip inflexibility. If your baby likes to do this, make sure that you practice the following massage regularly.

1

Lay your baby on her back and hold her legs by the ankles. Make sure that her legs are relaxed by "bicycling" them around a few times—bending and straightening them rhythmically one after the other.

• *Continue for about 20 seconds.*

2

Now, clap your baby's feet together and let her knees bend outward.

• *Continue for about 20 seconds.*

3

Using your right hand, take your baby's right foot onto her tummy, so that her knee bends outward, and hold the foot down gently onto her navel. Keep your right hand in this position while you knead and rub her right buttock and the back of her thigh with your left hand. Do this for about half a minute and then slowly and gently shake your baby's leg straight.

• *Repeat the sequence with your baby's left leg.*

4

Take both of your baby's legs by the ankles and perform a few bicycles, then clap the soles of her feet together. Push both of your baby's feet down onto her belly. Gently hold her feet in place with your left hand, place your right hand on her lower back and massage around the base of her spine.

• *Continue for about 20 seconds.*

5

Gently shake her legs—bending them and straightening them— and finish by stroking down the front of your baby's legs from the hips to the feet, using the weight of your relaxed hands.

• *Repeat 4-5 times.*

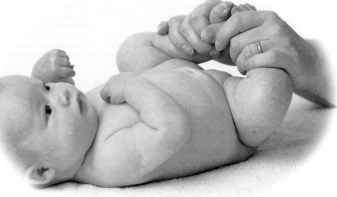

...to belly...

Every emotional feeling is mirrored by a change in our muscles and nowhere is this more apparent than in the belly—the emotional center of the body. The belly tightens in response to fear and anxiety and relaxes with tranquility. Lay your hand on your baby's tummy when she is relaxed and happy and it will feel soft and malleable; do the same when she is upset, and it will be hard and unyielding.

Massaging your baby's belly will help to relax her. It can also relieve stress, infant anxiety, and birth trauma. And a relaxed belly eases digestion, as it allows the diaphragm at the base of the lungs to descend, both increasing the volume of oxygen and creating a gentle internal wave that soothes the digestive organs with every breath. Massage of the belly can also help to relieve any colic and constipation.

Wait for the umbilical cord to heal before you massage your baby's belly and do not try to massage it if your baby is upset—instead try Tiger in the tree, page 84—a special technique for inducing tranquility.

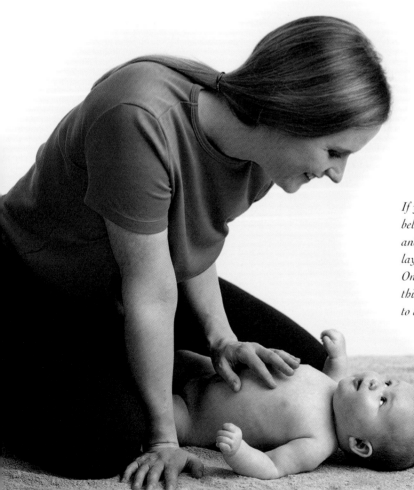

If your baby resists having her belly massaged, pat it, tickle it, and loosen it up first, then just lay your hand on it briefly. Once your baby has accepted this contact, you can progress to a full massage.

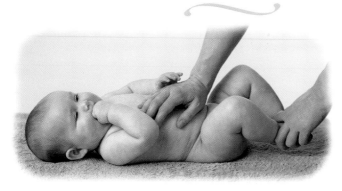

1

Using just the weight of your relaxed hand, massage clockwise, from your left to your right, in a circular motion—the same direction as food passing through the digestive system.

• *Repeat 4–5 times.*

2

Place your cupped hand horizontally across your baby's belly and push gently from side to side between the hips and the lower ribs. Never push downward on the belly, as this can cause extreme discomfort.

• *Continue for about 20 seconds.*

3

Massage hand-over-hand, from between the hip and lower ribs on the left of your baby's body, downward and across to just below the navel.

• *Repeat several times on each side.*

4

Repeat the first part of the massage with your cupped hand moving clockwise around your baby's belly and, this time, as your hand sweeps above the pubic bone, below the navel, lift your fingers so that the heel of your hand bears down with just a little more pressure. This is where the bladder and the lowest part of the colon is situated, so do not be surprised if your baby urinates. Any wind or waste that is trapped in the lower bowel may also be released.

• *Continue for about 20 seconds.*

...to chest...

A regular chest massage allows your baby to relax and breathe more deeply—leaving her feeling healthy and energized.

Oxygen is the very spirit of life and the deeper we breathe, the better we feel. As adults, when we receive an emotional or physical shock, we spontaneously take a deep breath or "gasp" and when we are in a state of stress (marked by a shallow, rapid breathing rhythm) we take controlled breaths in order to calm down. This helps us to maintain a feeling of relaxation and wellbeing as the cells of our bodies receive a plentiful supply of revitalizing oxygen.

Your baby's abdominal breathing rhythm is intuitively healthy—her lower ribs and belly expand on the in-breath as she fills her lungs with air and they contract in harmony as she empties them. And your young baby will start to open her chest even more fully when she stretches open her arms and begins to strengthen and straighten her back in preparation for upright postures and mobility.

You can encourage her to maintain her healthy breathing rhythm and reap the benefits of abdominal breathing. An open chest and a relaxed breathing rhythm will sustain your baby's growth and development and help in her resistance to and recovery from illness and infection.

In addition, muscular tension in the chest can result from repressed or prolonged crying. By mobilizing your baby's chest and rib cage through massage, you enable her to breathe more deeply and efficiently.

1

Sitting comfortably, with your baby lying on the floor in front of you, place your relaxed well-oiled hands on the center of your baby's chest.

2

Now, using the heels of your relaxed hands, massage downward and outward around the lower rib cage and return your hands to the center.

- *Repeat 4–5 times.*

3

Place your hands on the center of your baby's chest and massage upward and outward over her shoulders and return your hands to the center again.

- *Repeat 4–5 times.*

4

Cup your hands and tap them lightly across the top and around the sides of your baby's chest in a percussion movement.

- *Continue for about 20 seconds.*

...to shoulders and arms...

A newborn baby keeps her arms folded and tucked into her chest or the sides of her body. She does not open them readily and it may be some time before she is willing or able to do so. In response to a sudden sound she will throw open her arms involuntarily and draw them back together as if in an embrace. This is the "startle reflex," which will gradually disappear between two and three months as controlled movement takes over.

Voluntarily opening the arms involves a degree of strength and coordination that takes time to acquire. During the normal course of development, your baby starts to open her arms downward, then outward and then upward. The outward movement opens and relaxes the shoulders and chest, while simultaneously closing and strengthening the upper back from side to side. Stretching upward—lifting the arms and hands above the head—opens the chest and closes and strengthens the upper back downward, from top to bottom.

Massaging your baby's shoulders and arms in the order of her natural development will ensure full flexibility of her shoulders and suppleness in the muscles of her arms.

Have fun with your baby while you massage—hold her hands and give her arms a little shake to loosen them up slightly.

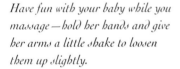

You can encourage your baby to open her arms outward by clapping her hands together very quickly to relax her before you open her arms.

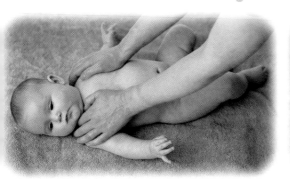

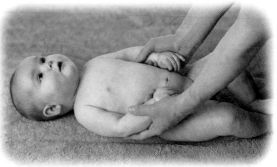

1.

Lay your baby on her back in front of you and, with well-oiled hands, work from the top of your baby's chest, moving your hands first upward and outward over her shoulders and then back down toward the center.

• *Continue for about 20 seconds.*

2.

Move your hands up and outward over your baby's shoulders and gently pull her arms downward—in line with her body—through the center of your palms. Keeping in contact, glide your hands back to the top of her chest.

• *Repeat 4–5 times.*

3.

Working from the top of her chest, move your hands outward over your baby's shoulders and smoothly pull her arms outward in line with her shoulders. Glide your hands back to the top of her chest.

• *Repeat 4–5 times.*

4.

Only when your baby is completely comfortable with the first three steps can you take the movement farther. Place your hands around the sides of your baby's chest, under her arms, and gently pull the arms upward through your palms, so that they are above your baby's head. Keep your hands on your baby's skin and glide them lightly back to her chest.

• *Repeat 4–5 times.*

...to hands...

As instruments of touch, our hands are the most wonderful organs of perception. When we speak of our sense of touch, we associate it almost exclusively with our hands. So much of the quality of our everyday lives depends upon the skillful use of our hands—we use them in a variety of ways—for holding, creating, caressing, and communicating.

A newborn baby has yet to acquire the strength and coordination to use her hands efficiently. If you put your finger into a newborn's hand, her fingers will close tightly around it—an

involuntary movement known as the "grasp reflex." Between two and three months, this will disappear and your baby's hands will be more relaxed and open. She will also develop the control to hold onto objects when they are placed into her hands.

It will be some time before your baby is able to judge distances accurately enough to reach out to grab toys and hold onto them— this usually begins to happen at about five months. And at around six months, your baby may be able to hold her bottle as she drinks, then begin to transfer objects from one hand to the other and, by seven months, she may be able to hold and eat a biscuit by herself.

It will be another two months or so before your baby is able to pick up small objects between her thumb and her forefinger and yet another two to three months before she can put an object in your hand and release it.

Massaging your baby's hands can be very enjoyable and, practiced regularly, it will help your baby to relax and open her fingers.

At around two to three months, you may notice your baby staring intently at her hands. She will begin to show a desire to hold objects before she can reach out and grasp them.

2

Now, relax her hand further by massaging her palm and the back of her hand with your thumbs and index fingers. Work from the wrist to the fingers, squeezing gently backward and forward.

• *Repeat 3-4 times.*

1

Start by opening your baby's hand and rubbing it between your palms.

• *Continue for about 20 seconds.*

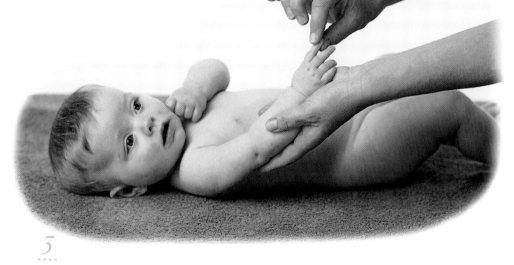

3

Spread your baby's fingers and thumb and, one by one, gently pull each of them through your thumb and forefinger.

• *Continue for about 20 seconds.*

If you use oil for this massage, make sure it is organic and wipe your baby's hands when you have finished—babies are always sucking on their fingers.

4

Now rub her whole hand again—back and front—through your palms.

• *Repeat the whole sequence with her other hand.*

...to back and spine...

The spine is of paramount importance in the body's skeletal framework—the head is supported by it, the vital organs are suspended from it, and the limbs are attached to it. The spine also houses the body's central nervous system, and is the source of all movement. The integrity of your baby's spine thus plays the major role in her health and fitness, both in childhood and as a grown adult.

Do not try to lift your baby by the arms during this massage—keep her arms low, alongside her body.

Your baby starts to prepare her body for upright postures in the first weeks of her life, but her back muscles really begin to strengthen when she lies on her tummy and gradually learns to lift her head. At this stage, your baby starts to "ground" herself on her tummy, and, step-by-step, she will lift her head, chest, shoulders, arms, and legs from the floor, eventually attaining a vital developmental posture known as "swimming." Massaging your baby through the natural phase of swimming will ensure that her back and spine are both strong and flexible, and that she develops excellent posture and a well-balanced body. It will also stretch the front of her body, to deepen her breathing rhythm and further relax her belly.

Kiss your baby's head and blow on her shoulders and spine from time to time—make the massage a playful time for both of you!

1.

Rub plenty of oil into your hands. As your baby lies on her tummy, massage hand-over-hand down her back—from her shoulders down the length of her spine. Use long, firm strokes, but keep your hands relaxed and make it fun for your baby, maybe giving her a tickle now and again!

• *Repeat 4–5 times.*

2.

Cup your hands slightly and pat your baby quite firmly all over her back and shoulders, and up and down the entire length of her spine. Everyone loves getting a pat on the back and your baby is no exception!

• *Continue for about 20 seconds.*

3.

When your baby can rest her weight on her arms, you can develop the massage. Put one well-oiled hand on the center of your baby's chest, and draw it back across the front of her left shoulder and down her arm a couple of times, taking care to keep her arm alongside her chest and not to lift it up.

• *Repeat with her right arm.*

4.

Place both of your hands on the front of your baby's chest and gently pull her shoulders back to open her chest and shoulders as far as is comfortable. Follow the movement through to pull her arms back, in line with her body, through the center of your palms, and release gently. Your baby will remain in this position on her own before her arms come forward and she rests on her elbows.

• *Repeat 3–4 times.*

...to head and neck

The crown of your baby's head fits perfectly into the palm of your hand and because you need to support it when you hold your baby, it is the most obvious place to massage. Soothing and extremely relaxing, head and neck massage can be done almost anywhere and anytime. It is remarkably effective, with an instantly soothing effect, while being completely non-intrusive. No prior preparation is needed: your baby does not have to be undressed and you do not need to use any massage oil.

Your baby's head has a number of fibrous joints called suturas which, due to their ability to move slightly, enabled her to pass through the birth canal. The fontanelle or soft spot left behind on the top of your baby's head is a strong membrane, but massage it gently, stroking with your fingertips and the palm of your hand. Some babies' heads are marked or bruised during delivery—wait for any obvious injury to subside before you begin to massage.

If you use oil for this massage, make sure that you wipe your baby's brow to prevent the oil from entering her eyes, as it may temporarily blur her vision. (Used regularly, olive oil can be effective for treating cradle cap.)

Sit comfortably with your baby on your lap and make sure that you are able to rest your arm at intervals during the massage.

1

Start by lightly massaging around the top of your baby's head in a circular direction with the tips of your fingers.

• *Continue for a minute or two.*

2

Then, stroke all around the crown of your baby's head in a circular direction using the relaxed weight of your palm and fingers.

• *Continue lightly for a minute or two.*

3

Now, using the relaxed weight of your whole hand, stroke all around the back of your baby's head, employing a circular motion.

• *Continue for about a minute.*

4

Continue the movement to include all of your baby's head. Stroke from the back of her head to the brow and around the crown.

• *Continue for as long as you like.*

5

Now stroke down the back of your baby's neck and shoulders and gently massage the back of her neck with your fingertips.

• *Continue for a minute or two.*

From head-to-toe

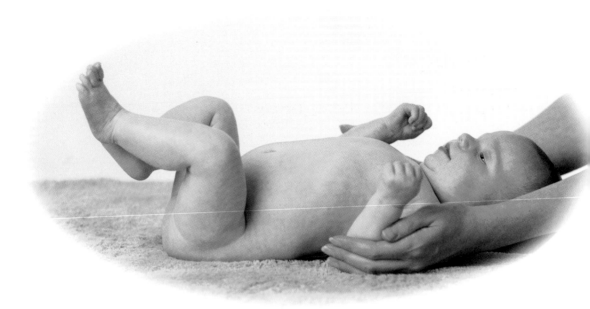

*The key to craniosacral therapy is
the lightness of the touch and the
alignment of the spine.*

At two months, your baby's arms and legs are beginning to straighten and at three months she can stretch out her limbs more easily. Encourage your baby to relax and "open up" her body with a craniosacral technique.

Unlike the toe-to-top full-body routine, this technique begins at the head (the cranium) and moves down through the body to the toes. This is because the onus here is on physical alignment and internal energy flow from the head downward. This technique promotes free-flowing energy by unblocking restrictions in the body's craniosacral motion—the movement of human cells. The brain and spine are surrounded by fluid, which moves in waves, and every bone, organ, and muscle also has a pattern of motion. Any blockage in the flow, usually brought on by tension, can be cleared by holding the head correctly and keeping the spine straight.

You need to choose the right moment for this technique—the best time may be just after the full massage routine, when your baby is completely relaxed and happy, or after your baby has had her bath—when she is at her least active.

1

Lay your baby gently on her back in front of you, with her head toward you. Sit behind her and, with your hands open and relaxed, slip your palms under the base of your baby's head and rest them on the floor like a pillow.

2

Gently position your baby's head so that it is perfectly centered, with her chin tucked into her chest to relax and lengthen the back of her neck. Hold your baby's head in this way for a minute or two until she is quite still.

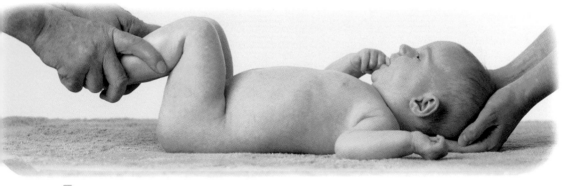

3

Once your baby is completely comfortable with this, ask your partner or a friend to help you to develop this technique. While you gently hold your baby's head in the same way, let your partner sit opposite and hold your baby's feet. Keeping them together, slowly bend your baby's knees to a right angle, with the soles of her feet facing your partner to ensure that her back is aligned.

• *Continue for about 20 seconds.*

4

Keep holding your baby's head as your partner gently shakes your baby's legs straight before stroking them lightly down the front from the hips to the feet. Talk and sing to your baby as you do this.

• *Continue for about 20 seconds.*

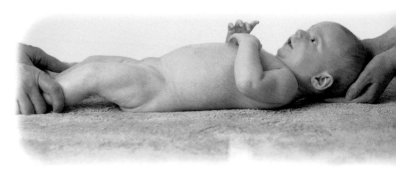

Air bathing

Babies need to spend time naked so that their skin is exposed to fresh air. Known as "air bathing" this is beneficial for maintaining the skin's health and resilience to infection. By regularly massaging your baby, you will also ensure that her skin is consistently air bathed, but even when you are not massaging, you can allow her to spend time naked around the house and, more importantly, outside. By doing this, you are allowing your baby's skin to absorb the life-sustaining, and healing properties of oxygen and absorb natural light—major components in the skin's production of vitamin D, which calcifies newly formed bone protein to create stronger bones.

Those times when your baby really doesn't want a massage aren't lost if your baby is still given the opportunity to enjoy a greater freedom of movement, unhampered by the restrictions of clothes.

Of course, you must make sure that the temperature is comfortable for your naked baby. If your baby is naked outside, ensure that it is warm enough, with no cool breezes, and if you are inside, choose a warm, well-ventilated room and keep her away from any drafts. Remember also that any oil on your baby's skin will intensify the effects of sunlight and cold drafts—so take care to supervise her at all times.

From two months, most babies love being naked. Bathing the skin in oxygen and light can also help to prevent and cure any minor skin disorders such as diaper rash.

Air bathing

1

Encourage your baby to hold her feet and suck her toes—look at the wonderful range of movement she has.

2

Use one of her favorite toys to encourage her to stretch out her arms and shoulders.

3

Let your baby lay on her belly so that she can stretch out and strengthen her back.

4

Once she is comfortable, she will strengthen herself even more by pulling her arms and shoulders back.

Securing your baby's posture

Key benefits

- Accomplishing a comfortable and healthy posture.
- Maintaining abdominal breathing.
- Aiding digestion.
- Promoting free and easy movement of the spine in all forward directions.
- Consolidating your baby's posture and helping him to develop confidence for sitting alone.
- Modifying your massage to accommodate your baby's increasing mobility.

The stages of motor development are universal and like the development of intelligence, each stage depends upon achieving the previous one. For example, your baby must sit before he can stand and stand before he can walk and so forth. The age at which he sits, crawls, stands, and walks has no bearing upon his intellectual potential and each child, being unique, does this in his own time. Some babies sit late and walk early while others sit early and walk late.

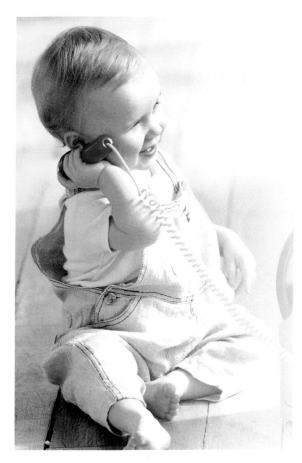

Sitting properly is an art, a major accomplishment for all young babies and like all other stages of development, your baby should not be pushed into it nor hurried through it. There is no prescriptive time span on sitting, so take your cues from your baby—your aim is to help him to secure this part of his development, to massage him through it so that he has the healthiest and most comfortable posture that he could wish for.

Continuing to massage your baby can become a challenge once he is sitting on his own. He may no longer be content to lie down for his massage now that he has achieved this stage of development. You will need to work with him to accommodate his changing positions so that he continues to reap the benefits of a comprehensive massage.

Helping your baby to sit

During her early weeks, your baby has little strength to support her head and neck and any attempts to pull her up into a sitting position before she is ready will result in her dropping her head forward and rounding her back. This is an uncomfortable and unhealthy posture, which will weaken her spine and can also inhibit breathing and digestion, so it is best avoided.

By two to three months, your baby should have developed the neck and shoulder strength to begin to work toward a healthy sitting posture. When she is able to lie on her belly with her head held up in line with her chest, she is ready to start the preliminary stage of sitting—with your help.

To sit comfortably for any period of time, your baby's hip joints must be flexible enough to allow her to sit on the back of her legs leaning forward. This position allows free movement of the spine in all forward directions. It also allows her chest to remain open to accommodate a deeper breathing rhythm and her belly to remain relaxed so as not to inhibit the rhythms of digestion.

Once perfected, your baby will spend many hours a day for many weeks sitting with a strong straight back. She will also accomplish many other skills in this position.

Sit your baby up—with her feet together and her knees open (this is known as "tailor pose"). Kneel behind her and slip your left hand around her chest so that she can lean forward into your palm for support, with her weight on the backs of her legs.

Now, with the fingertips of your right hand, gently stroke the crown of your baby's head to relax her.

• *Continue for about 20 seconds.*

Relax your hand, and, using your palm, massage gently all around the crown and sides of her head.

• *Continue for about 20 seconds.*

Stroke down your baby's back from the back of her head to the base of her spine with the weight of your relaxed hand. This will encourage her to transfer her weight downward onto the backs of her thighs, which in turn will elongate her back for a healthy posture.

• *Continue for about 20 seconds.*

Sitting supported

Your baby will gain strength spending waking time in the belly-forward position, and you will know when she is ready to progress from relying on you to sitting alone when she can lie on her belly and support herself on her forearms and hands. If she tries to sit unsupported at this stage, she could fall backward, forward over her feet, or sideways, so you need to make sure that she is supported from all sides.

In her favored position—with her feet together and her knees open, lean her forward over a long pillow or with a cushion placed over her legs and a cushion on each side to enclose her in a triangle. When your hands take the place of the cushions, however, you can help to massage her onward to the next stage of sitting, still ensuring that she is sitting well—on the backs of her legs.

Make sure that your baby is completely surrounded by padding as she sits in the tailor pose.

Never leave your baby unattended when she is sitting up with the support of cushions.

1

Take away the surrounding cushions and let your baby lean forward so that she is supporting her trunk on straight arms, for as long as she is comfortable. You can hold her lightly around the waist to steady her.

2

Now take your hands down and place them over her knees and thighs to stop her from toppling forward or sideways, while leaving her arms free to support herself.

3

4

Keep practicing this until you feel that your baby is confident and secure in this position, then you can continue the movement to consolidate her progress. Steady her with one hand and push downward on the back of her hips with the other hand to keep her "grounded."

Once your baby is confident in this position, you can begin to massage her back, stroking downward hand-over-hand, still pushing the back of her hips and the base of her spine downward.

Sitting unsupported

You will know when your baby is ready to start sitting unsupported when he can lie on his belly and support himself on his hands with straightened arms. At first, he will be unable to move in and out of this position without your help, but with a few weeks of practice, he will acquire the sense of balance he needs to sit for brief periods without using his arms for support—but he will still need some supervision. This is usually around the age of seven months.

When he is fully secure with sitting on his own, he will start to enjoy looking at the world from a new perspective. He will be able to reach for his favorite toys, he may be able to take a cup or biscuit, and he'll stretch his arms up to you to be lifted.

Massage here can help your baby to strengthen and consolidate his posture and to develop confidence in sitting alone. Learn to work with your baby, so that you can continue to incorporate elements of the full massage routine into your movements. You can modify some of the techniques for your free-sitting baby and concentrate on those that will benefit him the most at this stage.

This is an important time for your baby, so don't be too enthusiastic about hurrying him onto the crawling stage. Practice makes perfect and your baby will know when he has practiced enough to move on.

By kneeling with your baby in between your legs, you can offer him support —should he require it — as he learns to sit alone.

1

As your baby sits, kneel behind him and stroke down his back, hand-over-hand, and around the hips and top of his legs.

• *Continue for about 20 seconds.*

2

Stroke over his shoulders and pull his arms through your relaxed palms downward and sideways. This will help to improve his upper-body balance. You may want to use oil here, so that your hands glide easily and you do not pull your baby off-line.

• *Continue for about 20 seconds.*

3

Now, provided that your baby's belly is not full, give it a gentle squeeze and, with a relaxed hand, make circular strokes around the belly from right to left. Help him to maintain a relaxed belly now that he is spending more time in a sitting position.

• *Continue for about 20 seconds.*

Sitting Japanese-style

When your baby has fully secured the tailor pose and is ready to move onto all fours, he will lean forward over his feet and then pull himself forward onto his hands and knees. He may spend some time pulling forward and then rocking back into the tailor pose, but soon he will bring his knees together and then sit back between his feet—a traditionally Japanese position. This is an easy foundation for making the transition from sitting to crawling and your baby may now start to prefer this position to the tailor pose.

You will have to choose the right moment to massage your baby once he is in this position, because once he gets mobile, he will not want to remain still for any great length of time.

Some babies sit in this posture with their feet turned outward. If you notice your baby doing this, try to correct it by gently turning the feet inward—a much healthier position for his knees and hips.

Sitting Japanese-style

1

Sitting behind your baby, massage the front of his thighs—from the knees to the hips—stroking backward and forward with oiled, relaxed hands. This will relax his front thighs.

- *Continue for about 20 seconds.*

2

Now try to encourage your baby to lean back toward you at about a 30 degree angle. This will help to further relax the front of his thighs and will keep his lower back straight and strong.

- *Continue for about 20 seconds.*

3

Let your baby sit up straight again. Cup your hand slightly and, to relax your baby's belly, stroke from right to left with a circular movement. This can also aid his digestion.

- *Continue for about 20 seconds.*

4

Using oil, place your relaxed hands over your baby's shoulders and pull his arms outward smoothly through the center of your palms to help to secure his balance.

- *Continue for about 20 seconds.*

Mobility and soft gymnastics

Key benefits

- Encourages the development of back strength.
- Helps your baby to maintain good posture.
- Maintains the healthy functioning of the chest and belly.
- Encourages the flexibility of the spine and hips.
- Builds on self-confidence and a good body image.
- Encourages structural symmetry and balance.
- Promotes muscular relaxation, both at rest and in action.
- Encourages a confident physical relationship and emotional attachment with parent or caregiver.

Once your baby is able to sit up unaided, he will begin to move in and out of his first sitting position—then, as he moves from sitting to crawling, he will develop his second sitting position and go on to squat, stand, and walk. Having created a wide range of versatile movements, your baby will now start to strengthen rapidly and in carrying and moving his ever-increasing body weight from place to place, he will become a little "weight lifter." The more body weight he lifts, the stronger your baby will become and, like all weight lifters, unless he continues to make expansive movements he will lose some of his flexibility as he strengthens.

As your baby starts to crawl, stand, and walk, he will no longer wish to stay still for a structured massage, but the following soft gymnastic techniques allow you to continue to positively influence his development while he is on the move. They can be used for fun and games, while maintaining good posture and all-around structural fitness as your baby grows. And they will enable you to continue engaging your baby on a one-to-one basis, with lots of love and affection.

Like massage, these soft gymnastic games should never be forced or practiced against your child's will, and you do not have to do all of the exercises in one go. It is better to try them one at a time until you are completely confident and your baby anticipates and enjoys them. You can then aim to fit them in once or twice a week.

Encouraging mobility

Although most babies will crawl for some time before they stand and walk properly, some stand and walk without crawling properly. Usually, if babies miss the crawling phase it is because they have not spent enough waking time lying on their bellies and consequently they tend to be more reticent about moving onto all fours. These babies are often "bottom shufflers" and will move themselves around—often quite effectively—in a sitting position.

Babies that are used to lying on their bellies, once they are ready to begin crawling, will pull themselves forward from the first sitting position—tailor pose—onto all fours. From here, first attempts at crawling often result in the baby moving

backward and after some practice she will begin to pull herself forward using her arms and hands. After this, the baby usually begins to crawl around on her hands and knees, but some babies will crawl on their hands and feet like bears.

At the same time as your baby makes her early attempts at crawling, she will develop her second sitting position and may begin to stand with support. As she develops strength and confidence, she will start to pull herself up from squatting to standing, with support, and practice lifting her legs. Once she is able to lift and lower one leg at a time, she will begin to enjoy walking sideways around furniture, and then walking forward holding your hands.

There are many ways in which you can engage your baby at this time to encourage self-confidence and help her to achieve her full potential as she becomes mobile.

Preparing

Once your baby is sitting independently, kneel on the floor and sit him over your thigh. Let him squat and stand with his feet either side of your thigh. This position keeps his hips, knees, and ankles in line to encourage postural symmetry.

• *Continue for as long as you and your baby are comfortable.*

Crawling

To encourage your baby to crawl, rock him to and fro over your thigh, in an all-fours position.

• *Continue for as long as you and your baby are comfortable.*

Standing

Put her on her feet and hold her by the waist. Bear down gently, giving her the weight of your hands for stronger roots and better balance. You can develop this by taking your hands to her thighs and bearing down.

• *Continue for as long as you and your baby are comfortable.*

Walking

Once your baby is standing, you can encourage him to walk. Sit on the floor, opposite your partner—you should be close enough to touch each other's outstretched hands. With your baby standing in between you, you can call his name to encourage him to walk between you.

• *Continue for as long as you and your baby are having fun.*

Tailor pose swing

When most adults sit on the floor, they tend to curve their spines and their weight is supported by their lower backs. This sitting position is not only uncomfortable to maintain for any length of time, but it is also damaging to the back and the spine and can inhibit the necessary functions of breathing and digestion.

By practicing the technique described here, your baby will build up the strength and flexibility that are necessary to enable him to continue to sit with his weight on the back of his thighs. This will take the strain off his lower back and help him to maintain a good sitting posture. Your baby's internal organs also benefit directly because in this position his chest is more open and his tummy is relaxed, allowing him to breathe more deeply and encouraging a healthy digestive rhythm.

This position is also practical for your developing baby—by maintaining flexibility, his spine is free to bend from his hip joints, allowing him to reach forward in all directions for his favorite toys.

As your baby progresses from sitting to standing, he may lose some of his flexibility and with it, his perfect sitting posture. It is important, therefore, to keep using this swing to ensure that your child's hips remain flexible and that he retains a healthy and attractive posture as he grows and develops.

The swing will soon become a game that your child will actively enjoy and look forward to—you may find that if you forget to do it, he will be quick to remind you.

Throughout this soft gymnastic game, make sure that your arms remain under your baby's arms and over his legs.

This is your baby's first sitting position—with his feet together and knees open, his legs and hips are in perfect symmetry.

Tailor pose swing

1

Sit your baby on your lap in tailor pose with your arms under his arms and over his legs. Bring the soles of his feet together and pull them into the trunk of his body. Clap his feet together and slowly rock your baby from side to side.

- *Continue for about 20 seconds.*

2

Now raise yourself off your heels and support your baby by holding his ankles. Your baby will be held securely between your forearms.

3

Now start to swing your baby gently from side to side. Do this five or six times—as your baby finds his rhythm he will relax and begin to enjoy it. Continue to swing and now let your baby lean forward, taking his chest toward his feet. Make sure that your arms remain under your baby's arms throughout the exercise.

- *Continue for 4–5 swings.*

Strong, flexible legs

As the roots of your baby's body, his legs must be strong enough to both support and carry it, as well as supple enough to enable a wide range of movement from sitting and standing, to jumping and running. When your baby begins to explore his range of movement and starts to "find his feet," he will become increasingly confident and a little more independent.

As your baby's legs strengthen, he will no longer stand and walk with his legs and feet open "cowboy style" because his inside thigh muscles will contract and draw them in line with his hips. At the same time, other postural muscles—such as the calves, front thighs, and buttocks—will strengthen to make his legs more stable. If these muscles strengthen without being stretched, your baby can lose a degree of his body's range of movement. For example, he will no longer be able to take his foot to his face or enjoy the freedom of movement in tailor pose.

Your baby has spent a great deal of time and effort establishing a wide range of movement and it makes good sense to help him to retain this as he gains strength. Playing these soft gymnastic games once or twice a week will ensure that your baby maintains flexible joints and continues to enjoy a wide variety of movement and good posture.

You can help to maintain the flexibility of your baby's hips by sitting with him so that his legs are outstretched around your waist.

1

Sit your baby on your thighs and lean back slightly as you take your baby's feet to his face. Rock him from side to side and sing to him.

• *Continue for about half a minute.*

2

Hold one of your baby's legs from the back of the thigh and knee, and let the other leg straighten. Rub and massage the back of the thigh as you continue to rock and sing.

• *Continue for half a minute. Repeat with his other leg.*

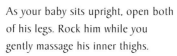

3

Let your baby sit between your knees in "side-splits"— with his legs and feet open. Close one leg in a half tailor pose, then straighten it and close the other.

• *Repeat this movement from leg to leg rhythmically for about half a minute.*

4

As your baby sits upright, open both of his legs. Rock him while you gently massage his inner thighs.

• *Continue for 20–30 seconds.*

5

Gently bring your baby's legs together and, keeping his legs straight, extend his heels by turning his feet out.

• *Hold for a few seconds.*

An open chest and shoulders

Unlike adults, who usually restrict their breathing to their chests and inhibit their emotional expressions to facial and hand movements, the child expresses herself with her whole body—jumping up and down and throwing open her arms with delight or shaking her fists and stamping her feet with rage. Babies are active, their responses are spontaneous, and their breathing rhythm is full and easy.

Young children have an intuitive understanding of the intimate relationship between feeling, breathing, and movement. As well as expressing their emotions with uninhibited movement, to suppress feeling—to subdue fear or acute anxiety—they will make themselves motionless, become very still, and hold their breath.

Observe how your baby sits and stands. Her straight back, free chest, and relaxed shoulders reveal a positive attitude to life and a state of mind untainted by negativity. Look how your baby breathes, every breath descending deep into her belly—her chest and abdomen working in harmony, expanding and contracting together.

Your baby's straight back and her open chest and shoulders illustrate the structural balance of her posture, where weight is easily carried and transferred bone upon bone without undue stress being placed upon the muscles. This allows the muscles to function healthily, to retain a high degree of relaxation even when the body is mobile.

Even from an early age, babies enjoy arching their backs and it is this intuitive movement that contributes greatly to a healthy posture and breathing rhythm.

This exercise encourages full relaxation throughout the front of your baby's body and strengthens her back and spine.

1

Sit on the floor against a wall or on the edge of a cushion with your legs straight. When you are comfortable, sit your baby across your lap, so that she is facing to one side.

2

Now let your baby lay back over your thighs, so that her feet remain on the floor and her head and back are arched. To encourage this movement, rock your baby gently and slowly "roll" your legs from side to side while you sing to her.

3

Once your baby is relaxed in this position, pat her chest with cupped hands, rub her belly clockwise, and stroke down the front of her thighs. Keep rocking your legs gently as you continue this light massage.

- *Continue for about half a minute.*

Your baby will soon learn to anticipate the arching movement and will begin to lie back without much encouragement.

Back strength and flexibility

Children constantly engage in vigorous physical games and activities that often demand a wide range of physical movement. The flexibility of the spine and the strength of the muscles that support it are therefore of great importance.

Once she can stand, your child must secure her balance and will continually test the boundaries of her movements and the potential abilities of her body. This will undoubtedly involve the odd tumble or two, but because children are more relaxed than adults—both in action and at rest—the shock of impact when they fall generally passes right through their bodies.

You can engage your baby in the following soft gymnastic game once she is on her feet and continue for as long as you can lift her and you both enjoy it. Practiced once or twice a week, it will help to maintain and improve your child's suppleness throughout the front of her body, the overall flexibility of her spine, and the strength of her back. It is also of great benefit to your baby's posture and promotes all the physiological benefits of good health and the self-confidence that accompanies fitness and good posture.

This is also a trust game and one in which you turn your baby's world upside-down and then help her to center herself.

1

Kneeling comfortably on your feet, on a cushion, sit your baby on your lap, facing you, belly-to-belly.

2

Now, holding her legs securely around the sides of your body under your arms, place both of your hands on her back—one at the base of her neck, the other around her lower back, across her hips. Let your baby lean backward and gently open her chest and shoulders by pushing her upper back. Talk, sing, and rock her gently, keeping her fully engaged.

• *Continue for about 20 seconds.*

3

Now, lower your baby and let her lean back over your knees, and place your hands over her shoulders. Your hands must be on the insides of your baby's arms. Rock your thighs gently from side to side to relax your baby.

• *Continue for about 20 seconds.*

4

Making sure that your baby's legs can roll unimpeded, stand up on your knees, supporting her from over her shoulders, and let her roll backward through your arms.

5

When she has landed in a standing position, drop your hands down, hold her from around the hips, and bear down gently using just the weight of your hands to "ground" her.

Sickness and special needs

Key benefits
- Soothes common childhood complaints.
- Can comfort a generally cranky child.
- Helps you to combat various types of congestion.
- Allows parents to ease physical problems.

Many childhood ailments and illnesses render the skin "prickly" and hypersensitive and when your baby is distinctly unwell, she will not want to be massaged in the normal way. Quite often what a baby most wants and needs is to sleep and be held until the prescribed remedy becomes effective. In instances like this, when you find yourself lying or sitting comfortably with your baby, try gently squeezing and kneading her hands and feet and stroking her head lightly with your fingertips—these techniques are non-invasive and can be relaxing and comforting.

The same approach can be used if your baby is emotionally upset, especially if she does not respond well to touch, finds it difficult to relax and let go when being held, or cries easily.

In the following chapter are some techniques for more specific conditions, but none of these are meant to be used as a substitute for professional diagnosis and recommendations.

Babies with special needs can also benefit from massage and you can modify techniques or bring out certain elements of massage to suit particular needs.

If your baby shows symptoms of illness, such as a high temperature, listlessness and irritability, watery eyes or runny nose, always seek professional advice—a prompt diagnosis can hasten your baby's recovery.

Coughs, colds, and congestion

A young baby will only breathe through his mouth when his nostrils are completely blocked with mucus. In the daytime, this may not cause too much of a problem, but at night it can prove to be a major source of discomfort. When your baby sleeps, his breathing rhythm becomes slower and deeper and if his nostrils are congested, he will gasp for air and awake with a start. This can be quite disruptive, particularly if your baby has already established a sleeping routine. If your baby is congested, place him in a more upright position when he is sleeping. You can do this by raising one end of his cot by securely placing a book or telephone directory underneath—don't let your baby sleep on a pillow. And avoid giving him mucus-making foods, such as dairy products.

These techniques will show you how to relieve nostril and chest congestion, but they are not meant as a substitute for a professional diagnosis and treatment, rather as an aid to your baby's recovery.

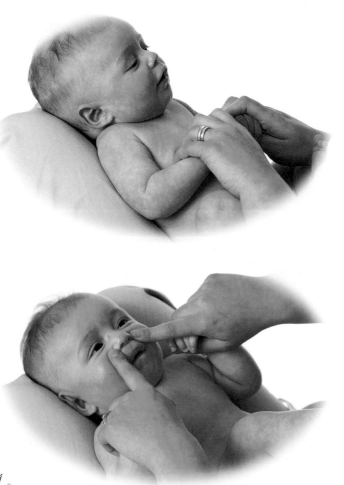

Nostrils

1

Sit on the floor with your back resting against a wall and your knees raised. Put your baby on your lap so that he is facing you.

2

Gently press your index fingertips into each side of your baby's nostrils and draw the nostrils open by pressing gently downward and outward under the cheekbones. You may want to try this on yourself first.

• *Repeat 4–5 times.*

Chest

1

Kneel on a cushion with your baby sitting on your lap facing you. Open your baby's legs around your waist and let her lay back over your thighs.

Some essential oils, such as eucalyptus and lavender, are recommended for clearing the sinuses. Mix 2-3 drops into your base oil.

2

Using the relaxed weight of your cupped hands, pat all around the center, and then the sides, of your baby's chest.

• *Continue for about half a minute.*

3

Now, place your baby on your thighs laying forward on her belly and, using the relaxed weight of your cupped hands, pat all around her back and sides. If your baby is heavily congested, she may vomit slightly following this percussion, as the bronchial tubes compress and expel the mucus.

• *Continue for about half a minute.*

Sticky eye

It is not uncommon for babies to have sticky eyes in the first day or two of life—this is normally due to amniotic fluid and other secretions entering the eyes at birth. In these cases, you can use a cotton wool swab and some tepid boiled water to cleanse the eyes— gently wiping outward from the inside corners. Beyond the first 48 hours, however, a sticky eye is due to infection and warrants further investigation. If symptoms persist, or if your baby's eye is bloodshot, you should consult your doctor.

An eye that is continuously sticky and watery can be due to a blocked tear duct. The tear ducts are lined with mucus membrane, an extension of the mucus that lines the nostrils. When this membrane becomes inflamed and swollen, the tear ducts become blocked, causing tears to flow from the eyes rather than drain into the nose as they usually do. Try this simple technique to clear the blockage.

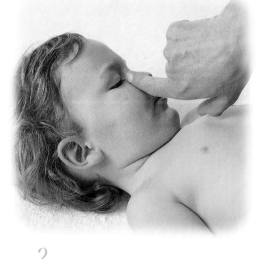

1

The tear glands and ducts are located in the depression in the nasal bone in the corner of the eye and run down the side of the bridge of the nose. Place your index finger outside the corner of your baby's eye and press gently into the side of the nose. You may need to steady your baby's head with your free hand while you do this.

Do not use oil for this technique as it can enter your baby's eye. Make sure that your hands are thoroughly cleaned and that your fingernails cannot scratch your baby.

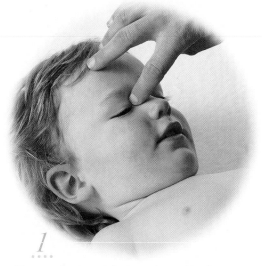

2

Draw your finger downward, along the side of your baby's nostril and under the cheekbone.

• *Repeat 3–4 times.*

Glue ear

If your baby has any ear discharge, other than wax, or experiences any ear pain, you should consult your doctor immediately. A runny ear should also receive immediate attention because it could be due to a middle ear infection that is causing pus to break through your baby's eardrum.

Glue ear refers to the discharge of a sticky glue-like substance in the middle ear, which prevents the eardrum from moving normally and can cause partial deafness. This condition generally arises from small canals—the Eustachian tubes—that lead from the back of the throat to the middle ear. The purpose of these canals is to equalize pressure on the eardrums—you can feel this when you swallow hard and when your ears "pop."

Glue ear can sometimes be treated by a competent cranial osteopath, but, as a preventive measure, try the following sequence when you massage your baby's head and neck. You may wish to use some oil to make the movement smoother.

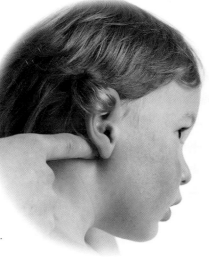

1

With your baby facing away from you, place your index fingers on the side of his head, behind the lobes of his ears.

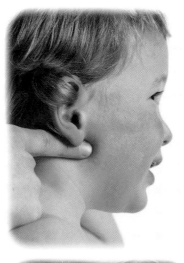

2

Press your fingers gently into the sides of your baby's upper jawbone, behind his ears, and draw them downward around the edge of the jawbone and toward his throat.

• *Repeat 3-4 times.*

3

Now, press your index fingers again behind the lobe of each of your baby's ears and gently draw them downward and toward you, around the sides and the base of his skull.

• *Repeat 3-4 times.*

Gas, colic, and constipation

We all take in air while we are eating and drinking, but because of the immaturity of your young baby's digestive system, air in the stomach or intestines can result in an uncomfortable pocket of gas. Positioning your baby correctly during and after feeding will help to prevent the build up of wind and also enable him to release it. Try to keep your baby's back straight while feeding and when he has finished his feed, pat him between the shoulder blades and stroke his back upward from the bottom to the top, while tilting him forward slightly. He may bring up a small amount of food—babies eat more than they need, so that their tummies stretch and they can go for longer periods between feeds.

If your baby has evening colic and you are breast-feeding, make sure that you are eating wholesome, nourishing foods regularly and that you are giving yourself time to eat properly. Sometimes, evening colic can result from you rushing your food and not eating enough at regular intervals. It is also not uncommon for breast-fed babies to go for a few days occasionally without emptying their bowels. You can use massage to initiate relief, but check with your physician or health visitor if you are worried.

It is better not to try to massage your baby's belly when he is distressed—try Tiger in the tree (page 84) instead. The following technique can be used between bouts of discomfort, when your baby is neither too hungry nor too full. A good opportunity for this massage is when you are changing your baby's diaper.

Giving your baby plenty of waking time on his tummy can prevent and relieve reflux, colic, and constipation as this position stretches and relaxes the abdomen, but do not do this immediately after a feed—let him digest his food first.

If your baby's belly is hard and unyielding, tickle it first and then just lay your hand across it gently before you begin to massage.

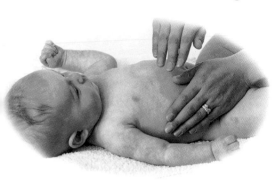

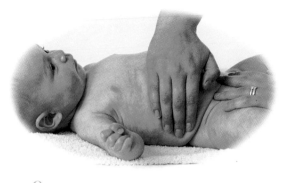

1

Lay your baby on the floor and, using the relaxed weight of your whole hand, massage hand-over-hand down the right side of his abdomen, from between the hip and the lower rib across to below the navel.

• *Continue for 2–3 minutes and then repeat on the left side of your baby's abdomen.*

2

Cup your hand and place it horizontally across your baby's belly. Squeeze gently and knead the belly from side to side. Don't push downward or your baby will resist and tense up. Keep it playful, so that his belly becomes soft.

• *Continue for about 20 seconds.*

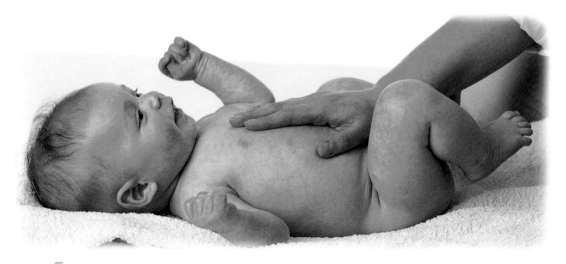

3

Now, using the relaxed weight of your cupped hand, massage your baby's belly in a circular motion clockwise from your left to your right.

• *Repeat 4–5 times.*

If your baby is suffering from gas, colic, or constipation, consult your physician. Check that your baby is not allergic to something in his diet—or, if you are breast-feeding, something in yours. If your baby has started on solids, try giving him pureed papaya fruit, which contains enzymes to aid his digestion.

Teething and irritability

Teething starts long before your baby's teeth make an appearance, which can be any time between three and 12 months. The first tooth is usually the lower central incisor and following this, other incisors appear—three up and three down, allowing the baby to bite. Altogether, your baby will cut 20 milk teeth—as opposed to 32 permanent teeth, which will start to appear only when she has reached about six years of age.

Cleaning your baby's teeth should begin with the appearance of the first tooth and should include the gums—you should clean your baby's teeth twice a day. Care for your baby's teeth should also include the avoidance of sugary foods and drinks. Your baby's teeth will rot quickly if you dip her comforter in syrup or give her sugar-rich drinks in her bottle.

Teething babies are often irritable, have red cheeks, and swollen gums. Sometimes they cry loudly and abruptly, as if for no apparent reason, and then stop as quickly as they started.

Many babies cut their teeth without problems with teething, but for those who don't, a homeopathic remedy, such as teething granules, can help. If your baby is experiencing particular distress, massaging her hands, feet, and back is non-intrusive and can comfort her when she is restless and upset.

Some babies salivate and press their hands into their mouths when they are teething.

There are many symptoms attributed to teething, most of which could also indicate more serious illnesses. If your baby appears to be unwell, seek professional advice.

A natural remedy such as camomile roman can be effective for soothing your baby during teething. Dilute a few drops in milk and pour into your baby's bath.

1

Sitting with your baby on your lap, squeeze and stroke her hands gently between your thumb and fingers.

2

Take the massage down to your baby's feet, squeezing gently and stroking both the tops and the soles of her feet.

5

Now, hold your baby close and stroke her gently all over her back and up and down the length of her spine. Talk to her softly as you massage her.

Sleeplessness

A newborn baby sleeps for regular periods throughout the day and the night, so she cannot help but interrupt your sleep. Having woken, if your baby has been fed and changed, she should return to sleep after a cuddle. Babies need physical contact—a baby's first home is her mother and a little time spent regularly in your arms is often all that she needs.

If your baby is clearly having sleeping difficulties, it is not advisable to walk around for hours in the middle of the night trying to soothe her. Tiger in the tree may help (see page 84) but if not, seek the advice of your physician or health visitor.

There are numerous reasons why babies resist sleep. If your baby is not hungry or uncomfortable and has stopped crying while she is in your arms but cries when you try to lay her down to sleep, she is clearly saying that she wants to stay with you. In this situation, a gentle massage can be enormously helpful for bringing about a successful resolution.

The following techniques will allow you to withdraw gradually, to offer your baby a loving touch that will reassure her of your presence and induce tranquility and sleep. If your baby sits up crying, lay her down and continue. Much of the success of this technique will depend upon you positioning yourself comfortably, persevering, and being consistent. Once your baby has accepted this, you will find that it will induce sleep, and that your baby will begin to anticipate it.

The same techniques can be used when you feel that the time is right to introduce a routine and put your baby to bed at a regular hour. You can begin to withdraw further by shortening the massage, but leaving your hands on your child until she is sleeping. When you have established this, you can reduce the time further and remove your hands when your baby is almost asleep—but remain within sight of her and quietly reassure her. The final step is to lay your baby down, stroke her, tell her it's time to sleep, and slowly withdraw.

Using this simple technique and a little patience, you will help your baby to drift off to sleep.

1

Lay your baby down on her side and stroke around the top of her back using the relaxed weight of your whole hand.

2

Now stroke down the length of her back in the same way as you would a puppy or a kitten.

This same technique can be used if your baby sleeps on her back—stroke her head, chest, and tummy in the order suggested.

3

Stroke around your baby's head, which fits perfectly into the cup of your hand.

4

Caress the top of your baby's head with your fingertips and withdraw slowly.

• *Persevere and if after a reasonable period your baby is still crying, repeat the whole sequence.*

Tiger in the tree

Your baby will probably fall asleep in your arms once her discomfort has been relieved by this technique.

Tiger in the tree is a wonderful position in which you can hold and massage your baby to relax her tummy and relieve colic, gas, constipation, crankiness, anxiety, and other ailments that are associated with acute abdominal tension.

The technique is both curative and preventative—it can be used on-the-spot to bring instant relief to your baby when she needs it most, as well as on a daily basis to help to develop a cumulative sense of ease that will dramatically improve your baby's whole disposition.

Your baby will experience a deep sense of relief and relaxation locally, in her abdomen itself, and because this area is an "emotional center," the sensation will then pervade her entire body.

Supporting your baby on both of your arms allows you to sustain the position for a long period of time, so that your baby enjoys the maximum effect of the massage. It is a useful technique for fathers especially,

because the baby is facing away from the breast and will not add to her discomfort by trying to feed. It also gives fathers the means to soothe a distressed baby when a mother is absent or needs time to herself.

Remember—the way that you support and touch your baby is important and has an effect on the success of the massage. It is vital to maintain your own sense of relaxation, even when your baby is distressed, by keeping your shoulders and hands relaxed and your breathing deep and rhythmic—your baby will sense your calmness and should begin to feel more relaxed herself.

This technique can be practiced with your baby naked or clothed. Its effects are immediate and it can be performed anywhere and at anytime. The more you practice, the greater the benefits.

Although this technique is highly effective, it is meant to complement, not substitute for, a professional diagnosis and means of treatment.

1

Hold your baby with her back to you and bring your left arm across your baby's chest, taking care to drop her left arm under yours so that you can comfortably cradle her head and neck in the crook of your elbow.

2

Bring your right hand between your baby's knees and place your palm flat over your baby's tummy, supporting her equally in both of your arms.

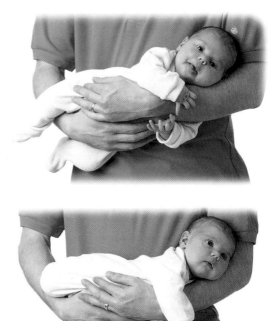

With your right hand spread, your thumb is on the ascending colon, between the hips and lower ribs, and your fingers are on the descending colon, between the hips and lower ribs.

3

Tuck your baby's foot into the crook of your arm and turn her over onto your hand. As she lies belly forward over your hand, very gently knead both sides of her tummy with your right hand. The weight of her body as it lies on your working hand adds to the efficiency of the massage as you are able to attain deeper contact without pressing in. Keep massaging for a few minutes. If your baby continues to experience discomfort, walk her around in this position and pat her chest.

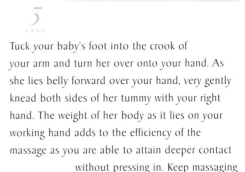

• *Repeat the massage on a daily basis and at frequent intervals.*

Cesarean babies

Babies delivered by Cesarean section with a total absence of labor miss the protracted contractions that accompany a normal delivery, and which stimulate the baby's peripheral nervous system and principal organs of survival. Consequently, these babies will benefit all the more from a regular massage. Combined with all the conventional benefits, a regular period of time spent massaging your baby will also give you the opportunity to strengthen your emotional bonds. This can be difficult at your baby's birth because of the medical attention that is required immediately after major surgical intervention. And as your body needs time to recover from surgery, physical closeness can be made more difficult by your inability to lift and carry your baby while your body is healing itself.

Following a Cesarean section, you can use some of your recovery period to lay with your baby and introduce the massage routine for the very young baby (see pages 16–25). By the time your baby is ready to move onto a more formal routine, you should be more able to lift and carry her. Until your scar has healed, it is best not to do anything that puts pressure on your lower abdomen. Once you feel able to lift and carry your baby, keep your arms as close to your body as you can. Never try to lift her at arm's length, as this will place enormous strain on your lower back and belly. Cesarean babies can be more prone to lethargy, so massaging your baby will give her the stimulation that she needs, as well as the opportunity for you to check and promote her structural health and engage with her in a unique period of emotional expression.

Use the time to bond with your baby and relax as you both recover.

Premature babies

Studies show that premature babies, massaged regularly for ten days, absorb their food more easily and gain weight faster than those who are not massaged. Consequently, these babies are more likely to leave the hospital earlier.

Given the high quality and sophistication of current neonatal care, most premature babies—some weighing as little as two pounds—survive. Some of these babies are fed intravenously and their heart rates, body temperatures, and blood pressures are all constantly monitored within a sterile incubator. Because of this, touching and stroking can be a difficult matter, but you can still make contact with those parts of your baby's body that are most accessible, starting with his hands and feet.

Very premature babies can be hypersensitive to touch at first, but once they have been allowed a little more time to mature, their mother's touch can be extremely beneficial.

A baby who spends a long period of time in an incubator can associate touch with medical procedures and may cry when handled. A sympathetic consultant will encourage you to touch your child and—when and where possible—hold and handle him to develop as much skin-to-skin contact as you can. Touching and stroking your child will help him to thrive, but don't look for an immediate response. Be patient—observe your baby and pay attention to his response.

At first, you could try just laying your relaxed hand or hands onto your baby's skin. The experience will be far more rewarding if you first gain his trust and then continue only when his responses are positive.

Visual impairments

To engage senses such as sound and smell, talk softly and keep your face close to your baby's as you massage.

Children with visual impediments can benefit greatly from a regular massage. Perhaps even more than most babies, these children have a profound need for tactile stimulation. The sense of touch can provide a means of communication that allows the child to receive surprisingly detailed sensory information about her external world and a means to interact with it.

The impairment of one sense often leads to the greater development of another and this is especially true of touch. Children who are visually impaired depend upon their sense of touch to give form and recognition to the objects in their external world. Given regularly, massage can bring you more in touch with your child. This can make it easier for you to guide her toward the objects she will use in her everyday life. It will also help her to overcome any resistance she may have to being touched and encourage her to be more socially interactive.

When you introduce massage, it is important to do it slowly. Begin by stroking your baby gently—talk to her and be attentive to her response. One mother I knew would close her eyes when she massaged her child. She would talk and sing and maintain a wealth of physical contact—stroking, kissing, and keeping her face very close to her baby's.

Hearing impairments

Babies with hearing impediments will benefit from massage. Given regularly, massage can encourage your baby's development, which may otherwise be delayed by his disability. It can help you to appreciate the ways in which he communicates and strengthen your emotional relationship—adding to your child's self-esteem.

A baby who has a hearing impairment needs to be talked to and given lots of visual cues, as well as plenty of physical expressions of affection. Speak to your baby and mouth the words clearly as you say them, so that your baby can focus on you fully.

Talk to your baby as you massage him. Stay close and use lots of facial expressions of approval and affection.

Introduce massage slowly and gently to overcome any initial tactile resistance. Stroke your baby and maintain eye-contact as you explain what you are doing as you do it. Keep the massage enjoyable and pay close attention to your baby's response.

Some babies with visual or hearing impairments are slow to crawl and walk. This may be because they are more resistant to lying on their bellies— they feel cut off from what is going on around them. When you massage your baby's back, try laying him supported on a cushion from the waist up.

Clubfoot

This is a congenital deformity in a baby's foot or feet, which twists the foot out of shape or position. One of the most common forms of clubfoot is where the baby's foot turns inward, often as a result of his position in the womb. This can be mild or severe and can sometimes be rectified by physical therapy or if not, by a minor surgical procedure. To straighten the baby's foot, the heel must extend. For the heel to do so, the calf muscle must relax and stretch to allow the movement. Here are some massage techniques that you can use, but check with your physical therapist before you begin, and show him or her what you plan to do.

1

Kneeling comfortably on your feet on a cushion, pull your baby's lower leg and foot hand-over-hand through your palms. With your thumb turned downward, draw your hand down your baby's calf. Follow through and turn the foot outward to extend the heel as far as it will allow without using force.

2

Hold the foot in this position while you massage your baby's calf with your other hand.

• *Continue for a few minutes or as long as your baby will allow. Repeat twice a day—morning and evening.*

3

Now hold your baby's foot in the same position as you stroke and stimulate the muscle on the side of his shin with your fingertips.

4

Sitting comfortably with your back supported, raise your knees and let your baby squat on your belly with his back resting against your knees. His knees should be flexed and open with his feet resting against your chest or waist. Massage your baby's calf while simultaneously trying to extend the heel by pressing his foot against your chest or waist.

• *Continue for a few minutes or as long as your baby will allow. Repeat morning and night.*

Support your baby as he rests his feet on your belly, so that he cannot propel himself over your knees.

Cerebral palsy

Make sure that you talk, sing, and remain close to your baby, so that she remains engaged.

This condition is attributed to a lack of development of the part of the brain concerned with movement and posture. Adjoining parts of the brain may also be affected, resulting in learning and visual difficulties including poor speech, hearing, and vision. The effects vary from child to child and range from slight to severe.

There are three recognized forms of cerebral palsy: ataxia—an unsteady walk with balancing difficulties, spasticity—disordered control of movement mostly associated with stiff muscles; and athetosis—uncontrollable or involuntary movements of different parts of the body. Children who are severely affected by cerebral palsy can require full time care and postural support. On a day-to-day basis, massage can bring a moderate to high degree of relief and an improvement in the quality of their lives. If you are not already massaging your child, enlist the help of your physical therapist and show him what it is that you wish to do.

Any improvement in muscle tone brings with it more potential for movement and can influence posture. Massage can relieve the cramps that result from stiff muscles. Chronic gas and constipation often caused by poor posture and the lack of movement and mobility can be relieved. Circulation can be enhanced and a regular period of one-to-one physical contact through the medium of massage will also improve communication.

Cerebral palsy can go unrecognized for the first year or more, so if you have reason to believe that your child may be affected, seek medical advice. If your baby has been diagnosed as suffering from this condition, the sooner you begin to massage her, the better. Obviously, never try to force open or closed any of your baby's joints—modify the techniques to suit your baby. If your baby resists being naked, massage her clothed. Introduce the massage slowly—maybe one part of your baby's body at a time. You could start with the hands and feet, then the hands and arms, the feet and legs, to build up a routine. Try to massage your baby daily and if you encounter any difficulties, consult your physical therapist.

Reintroducing massage

Increasing mobility and the urge to explore generally mean that most babies go through a period during which they resist laying still long enough for an "all over" massage. When this happens, don't undress your baby for massage, but whenever you are sitting together, continue to rub her back and her head, her arms, legs, and feet. Try to maintain this kind of affectionate touch whenever it is mutually enjoyable. Although your baby may not want to be undressed and massaged, the need to be held and touched is still tremendously important as your sustained physical reassurances will continue to add to your child's sense of self-worth and her healthy body image. Lots of spontaneous hugs, kisses, and strokes will add to your baby's self-esteem and will make it easier for you to reintroduce massage into your relationship when you think that the time is right for you to do so. When you feel the time is right, usually around 18 months, try to introduce the following routine.

You can continue to enjoy those moments of affectionate physical contact as your baby discovers new things about the world around her.

1

Place both hands on the center of your baby's chest and massage upward, outward, and back to the center with your relaxed hands.

• *Repeat 4-5 times.*

2

Rub your baby's shoulders gently but firmly, backward and forward from the sides of his neck outward.

• *Continue for about 20 seconds.*

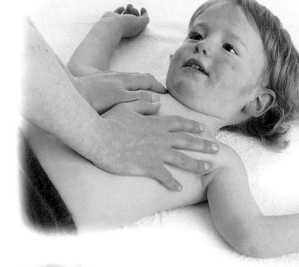

3

Keeping your hands on your baby's skin, stroke downward from the shoulders to the hips and back again.

• *Repeat 4-5 times.*

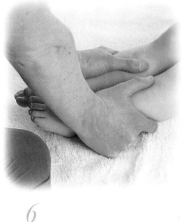

4

Using the relaxed weight of one hand, massage your baby's belly clockwise in a circular motion.

• *Repeat 5-6 times.*

5

Massage the front of your baby's thighs by squeezing and releasing and rubbing gently five or six times. Keep your hands on and repeat with your baby's calves.

6

Keep your hands on your baby's skin and stroke back up to his shoulders and right down to his feet.

• *Repeat 3-4 times, ending with the feet.*

A STRONGER TOUCH

The onset of the "terrible twos," from about 18 months, is the time your baby begins to assert herself and her quest for independence with more determination, and requires even more patience and understanding from the adults that surround her. Appropriately, it seems that around this age there are periods when babies once again enjoy being massaged and these interludes can often provide a welcome break in the emotional extremes that may prevail at this time.

Now that your baby is stronger and more resilient, you may need to add more depth to your touch and give a slightly stronger and faster massage. To keep your baby's attention, you must continue to talk, sing, and maintain eye-contact with your child as much as you can, for as long as you massage.

If you have been practicing the soft gymnastic games on pages 60–71, you may wish to combine massage with one or two of them.

Take opportunities to air-bathe your baby as she enjoys her mobility and use massage as a means of setting her on the road to independence.

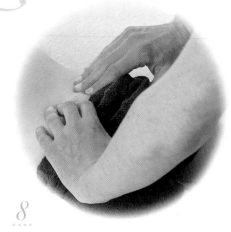

7

With your baby laying on his belly, rub his shoulders with your palms and massage the sides of his upper spine, pressing in gently with your thumbs.

- *Continue for about 20 seconds.*

8

Stroke down your baby's back from his shoulders to his feet, using the relaxed weight of both hands. Using your fingertips, massage the base of his spine and rub gently.

- *Repeat 3-4 times.*

9

With the middle fingers and index fingers of both hands, glide up both sides of your baby's back from the base of the spine to the back of the neck and back down again.

- *Continue for about 20 seconds.*

10

Now spread your fingers and draw the relaxed weight of your hands all the way down to the feet. Glide your hands back up to the base of your baby's spine.

- *Repeat 3-4 times.*

11

To finish, stroke down the back of your baby's body from shoulders to feet.

- *Repeat 3-4 times.*

Index

ACKNOWLEDGEMENTS

Shuana N'diaye and Roland Codd
for design assistance.

Picture credits: p. 17 Telegraph
Colour Library; p. 27 Telegraph
Colour Library; p. 50 The
Stockmarket; p. 51 Images Colour
Library; p. 60 GettyOne Stone;
p. 61 The Stockmarket;
p. 72 Powerstock Zefa Photo
Library; p. 86 GettyOne Stone;
p. 87 Steve Grand/Science Photo
Library; p. 88 GettyOne Stone;
p. 91 GettyOne Stone; p. 92 The
Stockmarket; p. 94 Telegraph
Colour Library.